IMPROVING OUR ENVIRONMENT

Waste & Recycling

Carol Inskipp

HODDER
Wayland

An imprint of Hodder Children's Books

Titles in this series:
Air Pollution
Saving Energy
Saving Water
Waste & Recycling

For more information on this series and other Hodder Wayland titles, go to
www.hodderwayland.co.uk

Series editor: Victoria Brooker
Editor: Margot Richardson
Designer: Fiona Webb
Artwork: Peter Bull

First published in 2005 by Hodder Wayland, an imprint of Hodder Children's Books
© Copyright Hodder Wayland 2005

British Library Cataloguing in Publication Data
Inskipp, Carol, 1948-
Waste & recycling. - (Improving our environment)
1.Recycling (Waste, etc.) - Juvenile literature
I.Title
363.7'282
ISBN 0 7502 4659 6

Printed and bound in China

The Publishers would like to thank the following for permission to reproduce
their pictures: Chapel Studios/Zul Mukhida title page, 27; Ecoscene Photo Library
(Jan Bower) 11, (Phillip Colla) 19, (Vicki Coombs) 29; Laurel Firestone 13; FPLA
(G Marcoaldi/©Panda Photo) 15, (S & D & K Maslowski) 24, (Mike J Thomas) 25;
Still Pictures (Thomas Rapauch) 4, (Jeff Greenberg) 5, (Martin Wyness) 8,
(J P Sylvestre) 9, (Dylan Garcia) 12, (Dylan Garcia) 16, (Hartmut Schwarzbach) 17,
(John Cancalosi) 18, (Andre Maslenmnikov) 20, (Andre Maslenmnikov) 21,
(Mark Edwards) 22, (Ray Pfortner) 23, (Argus) 26; Topham Picturepoint 6,
(Tony Savino/Image Works) 7; Hodder Wayland Photo Library (Angela Hampton) 28.
Cover picture: Bottles collected for recycling in the Netherlands by Getty Images

The website addresses (URLs) included in this book were valid at the time of going
to press. However, because of the nature of the Internet, it is possible that some
addresses may have changed, or sites may have changed or closed down since
publication. While the authors and Publishers regret any inconvenience this may
cause the readers, no responsibility for any such changes can be accepted by either
the author or the Publisher.

Contents

Words in **bold like this**, or in *italic like this*, can be found in the glossary.

Drowning in waste

Waste materials are those we do not need or want. All the time, people are throwing away leftover food, glass, tins, plastic, paper and old clothes; as well as machines such as cars, computers and fridges. We are also burning petrol, oil and coal and getting rid of many different kinds of man-made chemicals.

All over the world, people are buying more and more goods, and throwing away increasing amounts of waste. The world **population** is rising, so that greater numbers of people are adding to the mountains of rubbish.

weblinks

For more information about waste go to www.waylinks.co.uk/series/improving/waste

We are running out of places to dump rubbish. ▼

Some of this waste comes from **packaging**, wrapped around goods we buy. As well, many products we buy only have a short life. When machines such as washing machines or mobile phones break down, they are not repaired and end up on the scrap heap. Factories and mines also create waste products when they make the goods we need.

◄ **Household waste can be sorted into different types, such as paper, aluminium cans and plastic.**

KNOW THE FACTS

In 2001, an average American's household waste was more than twice that of a European and nearly seven times that produced by an Indian household.

The mess we're in

Earth, its *atmosphere* and all its people are being threatened by our waste.

Rubbish that is dumped or burned causes air and water **pollution** that is harmful to our health, wildlife and the **environment**. **By-products** from factories and mining can also result in pollution if they are not disposed of properly.

Waste from homes and factories has been allowed to flow into this canal in a Chinese city. ▼

Using up resources

Making and using new goods is using up the world's valuable **natural resources** (the living and non-living things that occur naturally on Earth and are useful to us, such as **fossil fuels**). If we carry on using resources at the same rate, there will not be enough left for people in the future.

Waste gases

Carbon dioxide gas (CO_2) is present in the atmosphere, and warms the Earth enough for us to live comfortably. When we burn fossil fuels, such as oil, waste CO_2 gas is produced. This is leading to more CO_2 in the atmosphere. As a result, world temperatures are rising and are causing changes to our climate. Around the world, there are more violent storms, droughts and flooding.

▲ Scientists believe that *climate change* is causing more violent storms and flooding. Storms can destroy homes, as in this trailer park in Florida, USA.

weblinks

For more information about waste go to www.waylinks.co.uk/series/improving/waste

Toxic waste

Much of our waste contains chemicals that are toxic: that is, poisonous. If not used carefully or disposed of safely they may damage our health or the environment.

In our homes, a large number of products that are part of our everyday lives – from paints, polishes, oil, **pesticides** and air fresheners, to computers and TVs – contain toxic chemicals. Factories and workshops also make toxic waste.

◄ Computers contain materials that are highly toxic. These find their way into nearby soil, water and air when computers are thrown away.

Where does it go?

People know very little about how much toxic waste is produced or where it goes. When released into the environment, toxic chemicals travel freely in the air, get into rivers and eventually reach the sea. They are absorbed by wildlife and humans through the skin or are taken in with food or water. More and more we are finding out that even very low levels can damage the health of people and animals, such as by causing cancer.

▲ Beluga whales in the St Lawrence River that runs between Canada and the USA are so highly poisoned by chemicals that their bodies are classified as toxic.

 **KNOW THE FACTS**

Up to 300 man-made chemicals have been found in humans. Babies now have *synthetic* chemicals in their bodies that have been passed on from their mother before they were born.

What happens to waste?

People get rid of waste in different ways: by dumping it in the ground, burning it, putting it in the sea, re-using it, or making it into new things.

Landfill sites

In many countries, most of the waste is dumped in big holes in the ground, or on waste mountains at landfill sites. While some of the waste rots away quickly, other types, such as plastics, may take hundreds of years to **decompose**. As the waste breaks down, toxic chemicals are often released. **Methane**, one of the gases that causes climate change, is emitted as well. Underground water and nearby streams can be polluted. Noise, nasty smells, dust and litter can create problems for people who live nearby.

Time taken for different types of waste to decompose. ▼

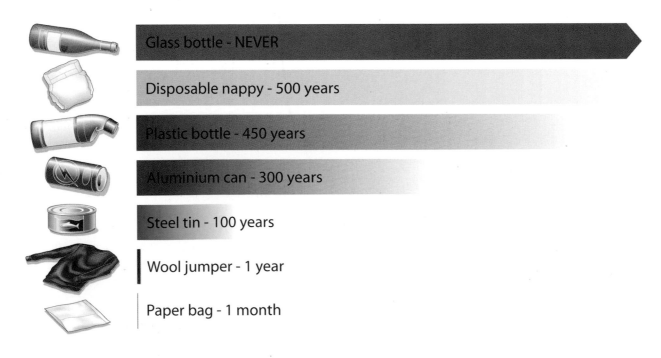

Glass bottle - NEVER

Disposable nappy - 500 years

Plastic bottle - 450 years

Aluminium can - 300 years

Steel tin - 100 years

Wool jumper - 1 year

Paper bag - 1 month

Burning

Some waste is burned and the energy produced can be used to make electricity, but the burning may cause serious air pollution. Scientists believe that this can produce gases that cause climate change.

Dumping at sea

Some wastes which are dumped at sea are toxic and poison sea life.

Recycling and re-use

Recycling means saving waste and making it into the same product, or a new product. When things are **re-used** they are used again in their original form and not remade. In most countries, only a small part of waste is handled in these ways.

▲ Getting rid of waste by burning is still widely carried out in many countries. This incinerator, a huge oven for burning waste, is in Hong Kong.

The three R's of waste

You can help to cut down rubbish by carrying out the three R's of waste: reduce, re-use and recycle.

weblinks

For more information about the three R's go to www.waylinks.co.uk/series/improving/waste

Reduce

There are many ways of reducing waste at home. The most important is to buy and use less. Try to hire, share and borrow things, rather than buying new ones. Choose goods with less packaging or buy goods in bulk. Take your own bag to the shops and refuse their plastic carrier bags.

Packaging on food creates a large amount of waste. Choosing foods with less packaging is one way of reducing waste. ▼

Re-use

Many things we call waste could be used again. For instance, you can re-use sheets of paper that have only been used on one side. Plastic **disposable** cups and food containers can be washed and used again. If goods are broken, get them repaired, or try to mend them yourself instead of throwing them away and buying new ones.

Recycle

If it is not possible to re-use items, recycling waste is the next best option. Making new goods from recycled ones takes less energy and resources than making items from new materials. Try to buy recycled goods instead of brand new ones too.

▲ In many countries, some people find waste that can be recycled or re-used as their job. This boy in Brazil is sorting plastic for recycling.

HELPING OUT

Hold a recycled art competition in your school. Create art with recycled materials as well as flat pictures. Use the competition to remind students and teachers to recycle.

What can we recycle?

Almost any item of rubbish in your home or school can be recycled.

How does recycling work?

People collect materials that can be recycled. Some homes have recycling boxes that are emptied regularly. As well people can take rubbish to enormous bins called recycling banks. The materials for recycling are then used to make new products and materials.

Same products

Many materials can be remade into the same products, such as **aluminium** cans, steel tins, glass bottles and paper.

There are many materials that can be recycled rather than thrown away. ▼

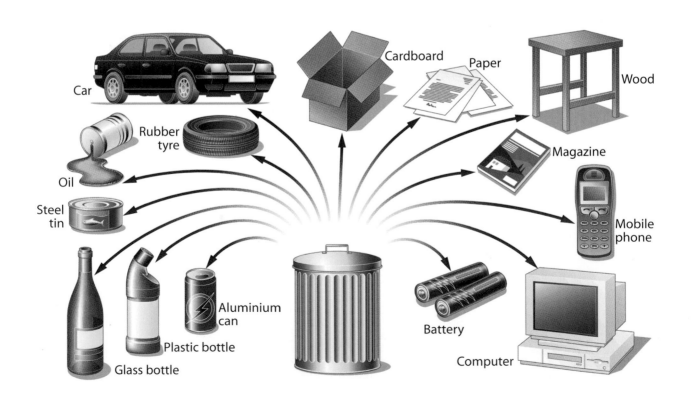

Car

Rubber tyre

Oil

Steel tin

Glass bottle

Plastic bottle

Aluminium can

Battery

Cardboard

Paper

Wood

Magazine

Mobile phone

Computer

New products

Other items can be recycled into completely different products. Recycled plastics can be made into 'fleece' for clothing. Rubber tyres have a huge number of uses: they are used to make bumpers, crash barriers and mats, burned to make oil and gas, and are even used to make shoes.

▲ Warm fleece clothing is made from recycled plastic. Five recycled drink bottles make enough fibre for one fleece jacket.

TRY THIS!

Recycling list

Find at least ten newspaper or magazine pictures of things that are often thrown away. For example, drink bottles, books, clothing, paint, cars, furniture, toys. Try to make a list of materials they are made of. Could any be re-used or recycled?

weblinks

For more information about recycling go to www.waylinks.co.uk/series/improving/waste

15

Working glass

Glass does not decompose if it is thrown away, but it can be recycled over and over again without any loss of quality.

weblinks

For more information about recycling glass go to www.waylinks.co.uk/series/improving/waste

Glass is made from sand, a chemical called sodium carbonate, and limestone, which are mixed together and heated to very high temperatures. Glass is ideal packaging for food and drinks because it preserves the taste and freshness of its contents.

Recycled glass bottles are often used for soft drinks. ▼

Six reasons for recycling glass

- Saves waste disposal costs.
- Helps save the countryside, so that waste glass does not go to landfills.
- Saves **raw materials**.
- Saves energy. The energy used to recycle glass is one-quarter less than that needed to make new glass.
- Cuts air **pollutants** produced by glass-making by over one-fifth.
- Raises awareness of waste disposal problems. Can be a first step in making people more aware of their environment.

▲ At this glass recycling factory, the used glass is broken into small pieces. Any bits of paper label or metal tops must be removed before the glass is melted down again.

 **KNOW THE FACTS**

Every glass bottle recycled saves enough energy to run a 100-watt light bulb for four hours. In the USA, most bottles and jars contain about a third of recycled glass.

Plastic planet

Plastics are all made from oil. Making plastic causes pollution, and when plastics are thrown away, they take hundreds of years to decompose.

Toxic plastic

Plastic litter is everywhere. It is even washed up on beaches of islands in the South Pacific where nobody lives. Plastic bags kill wildlife, block drains and clog up rivers. Waste plastics are part of the solid wastes that end up in landfills. As well as taking a very long time to break down, as plastic decomposes toxic **particles** pollute soil and water. Waste plastics are sometimes burnt, and then they give out poisonous gases.

Every year, in seas around ▶ the world, plastic bags kill an estimated 100,000 seabirds, whales, seals and turtles. This wild stork, in Spain, is trapped in a plastic bag.

▲ Four million plastic detergent containers have been recycled into *'plastic lumber'* to provide a new boardwalk and viewing system around Old Faithful Geyser in the Yellowstone National Park, USA.

Recycling

Recycling plastics is more complicated than recycling glass, metals and paper because there are so many different kinds. Each needs different treatment in the recycling process. Plastics are labelled so they can be sorted and then recycled.

TRY THIS!

Compare packaging

Collect six types of plastic waste packaging. Write a list of alternative kinds of materials that could be used for the packaging, such as cardboard or paper. Would these be more environmentally friendly?

 KNOW THE FACTS

The USA recycles 18% of all its plastic bottles and containers, and 36% of its soft drink bottles in a year. This saves valuable energy – enough to power a city the size of Atlanta for a year. Even so, about two-thirds of US plastic ends up in landfills.

Saving paper

Paper plays a large part in our lives, but paper-making uses huge amounts of chemicals, energy and water, and creates air and water pollution.

Nearly three-quarters of the world's paper is used up by less than a fifth of the world's population, in the USA, Europe and Japan. The level of paper use is expected to increase by half, by 2010.

Losing forests

Cutting down trees for paper-making is helping to destroy the Earth's forests. More than 40 per cent of trees cut down are used for paper. An area of natural forest half the size of the UK is being lost every year. This loss of forests is **unsustainable** because the forests are not being replaced.

For logging to be sustainable, every time a tree is cut down, another tree must be planted. ▼

Paper and the three R's

Reducing paper use, and re-using or recycling paper, can greatly reduce harmful effects on the environment. Compared to other materials, it is easy to recycle paper. Almost any paper can be recycled, including used newspapers, cardboard, packaging, stationery and wrapping paper. Paper can only be recycled five to seven times, though, as each time it is recycled the paper fibres become shorter. In the end, they are too short to make good paper.

◄ When it is being recycled, old paper is shredded into small pieces. Then it is made into pulp with water, and the pulp is made into new paper.

Aluminium can recycling

Aluminium is expensive to produce, but easy to recycle. It can be recycled forever without any loss in quality.

Aluminium comes from a rock called bauxite. The bauxite is mined and then melted down to extract the aluminium. A very large amount of energy is needed to obtain aluminium. Huge quantities of waste pollutants are produced including mud and carbon dioxide (CO_2), the main gas causing climate change. As a result, in some countries, mining and **smelting** aluminium is causing high levels of environmental damage.

When bauxite is turned into aluminium, huge amounts of wastes are produced: 1.5 tonnes of red mud, as in this tank of waste _slurry,_ and 360 kg of solid wastes for each tonne of aluminium. ▼

▲ Recycling companies make money from the waste materials they collect. Aluminium cans are worth five times more than glass or plastic bottles.

Recycling cans

Aluminium drinks cans are the most valuable containers to recycle. The energy saved by making aluminium cans from recycled aluminium is nearly 95 per cent. As well, recycling aluminium produces 95 per cent less air and water pollution than making aluminium to start with. The world leader in can recycling is Brazil, where 87 per cent of cans were recycled in 2002.

KNOW THE FACTS

In 2002 over half of the USA's aluminium cans were recycled, making it the most recycled item in the USA. However, if you stacked the aluminium cans that are sent to landfills in the USA, in just five weeks they would reach the moon!

Making compost

Garden and kitchen wastes make up over a third of all household rubbish. However, it is easy to turn it into compost which is good for gardens and growing more food.

weblinks

For more information about composting go to www.waylinks.co.uk/series/improving/waste

Kitchen and garden rubbish, called **organic waste**, can be particularly nasty. It smells bad and attracts pests, such as rats. When dumped as landfill it gradually breaks down, but if there is not enough oxygen it produces methane, a gas that contributes to climate change. Methane can also cause fires and explosions.

Kitchen rubbish often attracts pests. These racoons in Ohio, USA, raid a bin for a tasty snack. ▼

The best way to make compost is to pile up layers of green garden waste, kitchen waste and garden soil. It takes about three months to rot down to a crumbly, earthy mixture. People who don't have much outdoor space sometimes use a large plastic composting bin or even a plastic wormery, where worms eat their way through the rubbish.

▲ **Making compost at home reduces the amount of rubbish that has to be taken away and landfill sites become safer and easier to manage.**

TRY THIS!

See how compost is made

- Place 5 cm of damp soil in the bottom of a tall glass or clear plastic jar.
- Place damp food, leaves and grass scraps on top of the soil in layers 5 cm thick.
- Repeat making a few layers of soil and scraps.
- Leave the jar open and place it on a window sill.
- Water a little every week and stir the contents to keep them moist.
- Keep watch and see how it changes.

Re-use

**Re-using things is an even better way
of improving the environment than
recycling them.**

Recycling is a good way to reduce waste and save natural
resources and energy. However, as items are re-made, some
energy and resources have to be used. In contrast, when
items are re-used, they remain in the same form and so
no extra energy or resources are needed.

▼ **Computer companies
are now working on ways
to find new uses for old
computer parts.**

Ways to re-use

There are many opportunities for re-using things. For instance, using plastic bottles that can be refilled for milk and soft drinks is the normal practice in Denmark. Customers drink the contents and return the bottles to the shop where they are refilled. Increasingly, companies that make computers are now taking back used equipment. Then the companies are re-using some of the computer parts to upgrade computers and resell them.

Industrialized countries have much to learn from **developing countries**, where a much higher proportion of waste is re-used or recycled. Shoe soles are made from car tyres, and cups and jugs from tin cans, for instance.

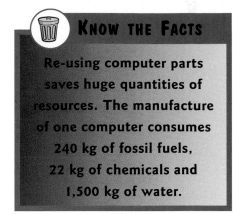

KNOW THE FACTS

Re-using computer parts saves huge quantities of resources. The manufacture of one computer consumes 240 kg of fossil fuels, 22 kg of chemicals and 1,500 kg of water.

◀ **This woman in Kenya makes money by repairing second-hand shoes. She buys old shoes, fixes them, then sells them to other people.**

Taking part

When you think of how you can improve your environment, think again of the three Rs of waste: reduce, re-use and recycle.

Reduce

You can reduce waste by thinking first before you put something in the bin. Do you really need to throw it away? An even better way of cutting down on waste is to only buy things you really need. Buying goods that will last a long time and don't break easily will help save waste and natural resources too.

By carefully choosing the goods we buy we can help to prevent waste and improve our environment. ▼

Re-use

Try to use containers again. Have printer ink cartridges refilled instead of buying new ones. Buy items such as drinks, food and washing up liquid in containers that can be returned. If you need to store something why not use jam jars? You can save egg cartons and margarine and ice-cream tubs for arts and crafts projects. By covering the name and addresses with stickers you can use old envelopes again.

Don't throw things out: give your unwanted clothes, books and toys to charity shops, jumble sales and community schemes.

Recycle

As well as re-using things, make sure you recycle more at home and at school. Remember to buy recycled products too. If your school doesn't have collection and recycling schemes ask your teachers to start them. Make your own compost from kitchen and garden waste.

▲ **Try shopping at jumble sales or car boot fairs – you often find a bargain!**

Glossary

Aluminium A strong, light, silvery-grey metal that does not corrode easily.

Atmosphere The gases surrounding the Earth.

By-product A second, less important product made during the making of something else.

Carbon dioxide A gas produced by burning, and by living things.

Climate change Changes in the Earth's climate take place naturally, but human activities are increasing the rate at which the climate is changing. The burning of fossil fuels, which interferes with natural balance of gases in the atmosphere, is largely to blame. As a result, world temperatures are rising and in the future we are likely to an increase in extreme weather, such as severe storms and flooding.

Compost Natural material that has decayed, which is used as a fertilizer for growing plants.

Decompose Decay; break down.

Developing country The poorer nations of the world, whose industries are less well developed. Developing nations include many countries in Africa, Asia and South America

Disposable Something that is intended to be used once, then thrown away.

Energy Power to provide light or heat, or to work machines.

Environment The surroundings and things that affect a person, animal or plant.

Fossil fuel A natural fuel that has formed from the remains of living things. Coal, oil and natural gas are all fossil fuels.

Industrialized country A country which has many different industries, and usually a good standard of living for its people.

Methane One type of gas that has no colour or smell, which burns if a flame is put near it.

Natural resources Natural living and non-living things on Earth that are useful to people.

Organic waste Waste that has come from living things, that is from plants or animals.

Packaging Boxes or wrapping around an object.

Particles Very tiny pieces.

Pesticides Substance for destroying insects or other pests of plants or animals.

Plastic lumber Plastic that is used in the same way as wood.

Pollutant A harmful substance that is in the environment, often put there by people.

Pollution Harmful or poisonous substances in the environment, such as in water or air.

Population All the things that live in a particular place or country.

Raw materials The basic materials that are used to make things.

Recycling Changing waste into re-usable material.

Re-used Things that are used again, or used more than once.

Solid waste Solids that we do not need or want.

Slurry A semi-liquid mixture, like thin mud.

Smelting Extracting a metal from rock by heating and melting. Aluminim is smelted from a mineral called bauxite.

Synthetic Something that is made by people; not natural.

Toxic Poisonous.

Unsustainable Something that cannot be continued without using it up or damaging it. For example, chopping down trees without planting new ones is unsustainable.

Further Information

Reading

Earth Watch:Waste Disposal by Sally Morgan (Franklin Watts, 2000)
Environment Starts Here!: Recycling by Angela Royston
(Hodder Wayland, 2001)
Green Files:Waste and Recycling by Stephen Parker
(Heinemann Library, 2003)
Where Does Rubbish Go? by S Tahta (Usborne Publishing Ltd, 2001)
Worms Eat My Garbage: How to Set Up and Maintain a Worm Composting System,
by Mary Applehof (Eco-Logic Books, 2003)

Campaign Groups

Friends of the Earth
26-28 Underwood Street, London N1 7JQ
Website: http://www.foe.co.uk

Greenpeace
Canonbury Villas, London N12PN
Website: http://www.greenpeace.org

WWF-UK
Panda House, Weyside Park, Godalming, Surrey GU7 1XR
Website: http://www.wwf-uk.org

Waste Watch
96 Tooley Street, London SE1 2TH
Website: http://www.wastewatch.org.uk

Zero Waste America
c/o Lynn Landes, 217 S. Jessup Street, Philadelphia, PA 19107
Website: http://www.zerowasteamerica.org/

Waste & Recycling Websites

http://www.epa.gov/kids/garbage.htm
US Environment Protection Agency – activities on garbage and recycling.

http://www.metrokc.gov/dnr/kidsweb/solid_waste_main.htm
King County, Seattle, KidsWeb – information.

http://www.earth911.org
Earth 911, US – information, games and activities.

http://www.wigglywigglers.co.uk
Wiggly Wigglers – information on wormeries

http://www.recyclezone.org.uk/
Waste Watch – information and activities for children, including
how to make a worm composter.

Index

Numbers in **bold** refer to illustrations.

32